"Look down upon me,
good and gentle Jesus,
while I kneel and ask you
to fill my heart
with faith, hope, and charity,
and sorrow for my sins.
Help me never to sin again.
I think of your five wounds
with great love and pity,
as I say the words of David,
"'They have pierced
my hands and my feet.
They have injured all my bones.'"

I, _____ ,

received my

First Holy Communion

Date April 14 1998

Church _____

Priest _____

Teacher Rivet

FIRST STEPS TO JESUS

A NEW PRAYER BOOK FOR FIRST HOLY COMMUNION

Edited by
RUTH HANNON

Illustrations by
RITA GOODWILL

THE REGINA PRESS
New York

Concordat cum originali:

Rev. Thomas Krosnicki, *Executive Secretary,*
Bishops' Committee on the Liturgy
Washington, D.C.

Imprimatur:

C. Eykens, *vic. gen.*
Antverpiae, 5 februarii 1981

English translation approved by the National Conference of Catholic Bishops and confirmed by the Apostolic See. Published by authority of the Bishops' Committee on the Liturgy.

Excerpts from English translations of *The Roman Missal* © 1969, 1973 International Committee on English in the Liturgy, Inc. All rights reserved.

Printed in Belgium

Cover picture by Fratelli Bonella Milano, Italy © ⚓
Illustrations © Copyright 1981 by Henri Proost & Cie Turnhout, Belgium

On your 1st Holy Communion

Foreword

My Dear Child:

This little book is written especially for you. It will help you to know Jesus, to love him and to follow his teachings.

You will learn how everything depends on the great love Jesus has for each of us. Never forget this.

May you stay close to Jesus throughout your life and may he keep you always in his unending love.

The Editor

*Love always
mom & Dad.
April 19/98.*

The Catholic Church

On Sundays and holydays good Catholics go to a Catholic Church. No matter how small or large, if the building be old or new, all who attend hear the same message, the message Jesus left for all men when he lived on earth. The message tells us how to live here so that we may find our way back to his home in heaven.

The Church is far more than just buildings. The Church is made up of people, men, women and children whose souls are marked with the sign of Baptism.

Even if all church buildings were

destroyed, the Catholic Church would be still alive. It would live in the hearts of its people. We call the love and devotion people have in their hearts for God, the invisible Church on earth.

A Prayer Before Mass

Dear Jesus, I am about to assist at Holy Mass. The Mass which will be said now on this altar is the same sacrifice which you offered for me and all the world on Calvary.

Give me the grace to offer our heavenly Father honor, glory and thanksgiving through this Mass.

May my prayers, through your sacrifice, bring blessings to all the world, everyone I know and all people everywhere.

HOLY MASS

INTRODUCTORY RITES

Priest: **In the name of the Father, and of the Son, and of the Holy Spirit.**

People: **Amen.**

Greeting ───────────────

Priest: **The grace of our Lord Jesus Christ and the love of God and the fellowship of the Holy Spirit be with you all.**

People: **And also with you.** *(or)*

Priest: **The grace and peace of God our Father and the Lord Jesus Christ be with you.**

People: **Blessed be God, the Father of our Lord Jesus Christ.** *(or)* **And also with you.** *(or)*

Priest: **The Lord be with you.**

People: **And also with you.**

Penitential Rite _____

After the introduction to the day's Mass, the priest invites the people to recall their sins and to repent of them in silence. Then one of the following forms is used.

Priest and people:

I confess to almighty God,
and to you, my brothers and sisters,
that I have sinned through my own
fault *(They strike their breast:)*
in my thoughts and in my words,
in what I have done,
and in what I have failed to do;
and I ask blessed Mary, ever virgin,
all the angels and saints,
and you, my brothers and sisters,
to pray for me to the Lord our God.

(or)

Priest: **Lord, we have sinned against you: Lord, have mercy.**

People: **Lord, have mercy.**

Priest: **Lord, show us your mercy and love.**

People: **And grant us your salvation.**

(or)

Priest (or other minister): **You were sent to heal the contrite: Lord have mercy.**

People: **Lord, have mercy.**

Priest (or other minister): **You came to call sinners: Christ, have mercy.**

People: **Christ, have mercy.**

Priest (or other minister): **You plead for us at the right hand of the Father: Lord, have mercy.**

People: **Lord, have mercy.**

At the end of any of the forms of the penitential rite is said:

Priest: **May almighty God have mercy on us, forgive us our sins, and bring us to everlasting life.**

People: **Amen.**

Kyrie ───────────────

Unless included in the penitential rite, the Kyrie is sung or said by all, with alternating parts for all the choir or cantor and for the people:

V.	**Lord, have mercy.**
R.	**Lord, have mercy.**
V.	**Christ, have mercy.**
R.	**Christ, have mercy.**
V.	**Lord, have mercy.**
R.	**Lord, have mercy.**

Gloria

We sing God's greatness and glory.

Priest: **Glory to God in the highest,**

All: **and peace to his people on earth.**
Lord God, heavenly King,
almighty God and Father,
we worship you, we give you thanks,
we praise you for your glory.

Lord Jesus Christ, only Son of the Father,
Lord God, Lamb of God,
you take away the sin of the world:
have mercy on us;
you are seated at the right hand of the Father:
receive our prayer.
For you alone are the Holy One,
you alone are the Lord,
you alone are the Most High,

**Jesus Christ,
with the Holy Spirit,
in the glory of God the Father.
Amen**

Opening Prayer_____

We ask God's help.

Priest: **Let us pray.**

(Everyone prays silently for a while)

Priest: **. . . forever and ever.**

People: **Amen.**

LITURGY OF THE WORD

We listen to God's message

First Reading _____

At the end of the reading:

Reader: **This is the Word of the Lord.**

People: **Thanks be to God.**

Second Reading _____

At the end of the reading:

Reader: **This is the Word of the Lord.**

People: **Thanks be to God.**

Gospel _____

Deacon (or priest): **The Lord be with you.**

People: **And also with you.**

Deacon (or priest): **A reading from the gospel according to N.**

People: **Glory to you, Lord.**

At the end of the reading:
Deacon (or priest): **This is the gospel of the Lord.**

People: **Praise to you, Lord Jesus Christ.**

Homily _____

We have heard God's message, and now we listen to the words spoken by the priest about God's message.

Profession of Faith _____

We express our faith in God

We believe in one God,
    the Father, the Almighty,
    maker of heaven and earth,
    of all that is seen and unseen.
We believe in one Lord, Jesus Christ,
    the only Son of God,
    eternally begotten of the Father,
    God from God, Light from Light,
    true God from true God,
    begotten, not made, one in Being
      with the Father.
    Through him all things were made.
    For us men and for our salvation
      he came down from heaven:
    by the power of the Holy Spirit
    (All bow at the following words
      up to: **and became man.**)

he was born of the Virgin Mary,
and became man.
For our sake he was crucified under
Pontius Pilate:
> he suffered, died, and was buried.
> On the third day he rose again
> in fulfillment of the
> Scriptures;
> he ascended into heaven
> and is seated at the right
> hand of the Father.
He will come again in glory to judge
the living and the dead,
and his kingdom will have no end.

We believe in the Holy Spirit, the Lord,
the giver of life,
> who proceeds from the Father and
> the Son.
> With the Father and the Son he is
> worshiped
> and glorified.

He has spoken through the
Prophets.
We believe in one holy catholic and
apostolic Church.
We acknowledge one baptism for the
forgiveness of sins.
We look for the resurrection of the
dead,
    and the life of the world to come.

    Amen.

General Intercessions (Prayer of the Faithful)

(After the priest gives the introduction, the deacon or other minister sings or says the invocations.)

People: **Lord, hear our prayer.**

(At the end the priest says the concluding prayer:)

People: **Amen.**

LITURGY OF THE EUCHARIST

Offertory Song _____

We bring bread and wine for the Sacrifice. Before placing the bread on the altar, the priest says:

Blessed are you, Lord, God of all creation.
Through your goodness we have this bread to offer,
which earth has given and human hands have made.
It will become for us the bread of life.

People: **Blessed be God forever.**

Before placing the chalice on the altar, the priest says:

Blessed are you, Lord, God of all creation.
Through your goodness we have this wine to offer,
fruit of the vine and work of human hands.
It will become our spiritual drink.

People: **Blessed be God forever.**

Prayer over the Gifts ───────

At the end:

People: **Amen.**

Invitation to Prayer ───────

Priest: **Pray, brethren, that our sacrifice**
may be acceptable to God, the almighty Father.

People: **May the Lord accept the sacrifice at your hands**
for the praise and glory of his name,
for our good, and the good of all his Church.

EUCHARISTIC PRAYER

The priest offers the great Sacrifice.

Introductory Dialogue _____

Priest: **The Lord be with you.**

People: **And also with you.**

Priest: **Lift up your hearts.**

People: **We lift them up to the Lord.**

Priest: **Let us give thanks to the Lord our God.**

People: **It is right to give him thanks and praise.**

Preface _____

Sanctus _____

Priest and People:

**Holy, holy, holy Lord, God of power and might,
heaven and earth are full of your glory.
    Hosanna in the highest.
Blessed is he who comes in the name of the Lord.
    Hosanna in the highest.**

Praise to the Father

**We come to you, Father,
with praise and thanksgiving,
through Jesus Christ your Son.
Through him we ask you to accept and
   bless
these gifts we offer you in sacrifice.**

Intercessions: For the Church

**We offer them for your holy catholic
   Church,
watch over it, Lord, and guide it;
grant it peace and unity throughout the
   world.
We offer them for N. our Pope,
for N. our bishop,
and for all who hold and teach the
   catholic faith
that comes to us from the apostles.**

Remember, Lord, your people,
especially those for whom we now pray,
   N. and N.
Remember all of us gathered here
   before you.
You know how firmly we believe in you
and dedicate ourselves to you.

We offer you this sacrifice of praise
for ourselves and those who are dear to us.
We pray to you, our living and true God,
for our well-being and redemption.

In Communion With the Saints

In union with the whole Church
we honor Mary,
the ever-virgin mother of Jesus Christ
   our Lord and God.
We honor Joseph, her husband,
the apostles and martyrs
Peter and Paul, Andrew,
(James, John, Thomas,
James, Philip,
Bartholomew, Matthew, Simon and
   Jude;
we honor Linus, Cletus, Clement, Sixtus,
Cornelius, Cyprian, Lawrence,
   Chrysogonus,
John and Paul, Cosmas and Damian,)
and all the saints.
May their merits and prayers
gain us your constant help and protection.

(Through Christ our Lord. Amen.)

Father, accept this offering
from your whole family.
Grant us your peace in this life,
save us from final damnation,
and count us among those you have
 chosen.
(Through Christ our Lord. Amen.)

Bless and approve our offering;
make it acceptable to you,
an offering in spirit and in truth.
Let it become for us
the body and blood of Jesus Christ,
your only Son, our Lord.

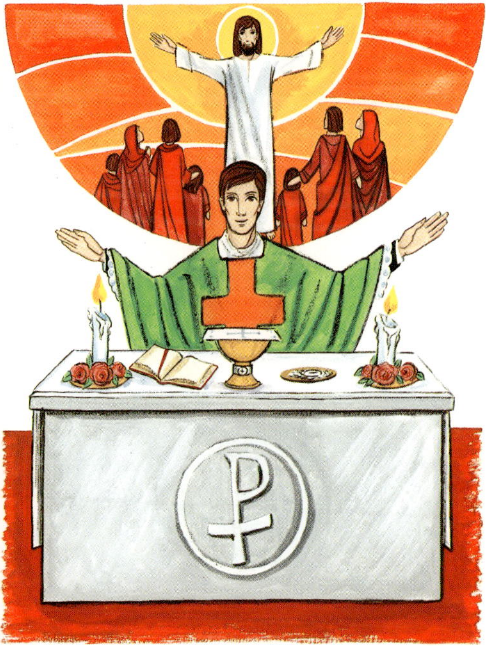

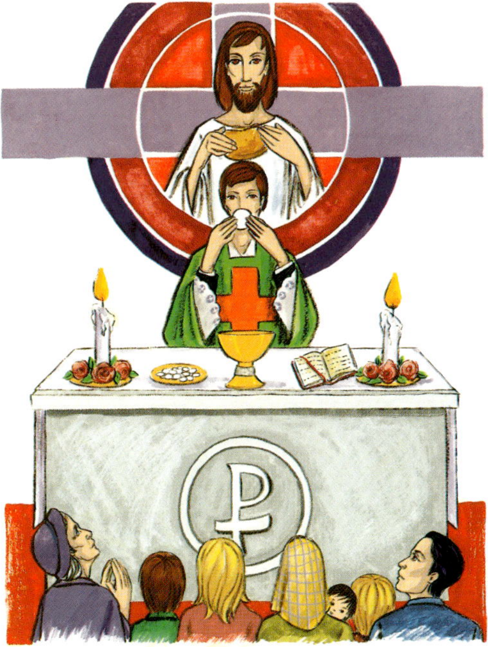

The Lord's Supper

The day before he suffered
he took bread in his sacred hands
and looking up to heaven,
to you, his almighty Father,
he gave you thanks and praise.
He broke the bread,
gave it to his disciples, and said:
Take this, all of you, and eat it:
this is my body which will be given up
   for you.

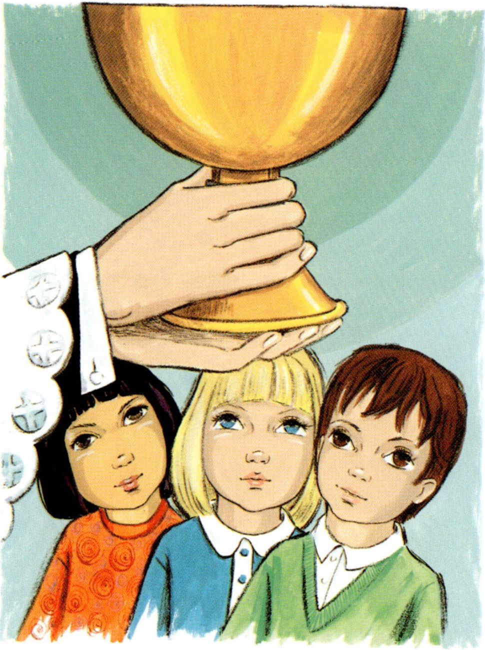

When supper was ended,
he took the cup.
Again he gave you thanks and praise,
gave the cup to his disciples, and said:
Take this, all of you, and drink from it:
this is the cup of my blood,
the blood of the new and everlasting
   covenant.
It will be shed for you and for all men
so that sins may be forgiven.
Do this in memory of me.

Memorial Acclamation

(After the words of institution, when the priest has replaced the chalice on the altar and genuflected:)

Priest: **Let us proclaim the mystery of faith.**

People: **Christ has died,**
Christ is risen,
Christ will come again.

(or)

Dying you destroyed our death,
rising you restored our life.
Lord Jesus, come in glory.

(or)

**When we eat this bread and
 drink this cup,
we proclaim your death, Lord Jesus,
until you come in glory.**

(or)

**Lord, by your cross and resurrection
you have set us free.
You are the Savior of the world.**

The Memorial Prayer

**Father, we celebrate the memory of
   Christ, your Son.
We, your people and your ministers,
recall his passion,
his resurrection from the dead,
and his ascension into glory;
and from the many gifts you have given us
we offer to you, God of glory and majesty,
this holy and perfect sacrifice:
the bread of life
and the cup of eternal salvation.
Look with favor on these offerings
and accept them as once you accepted
the gifts of your servant Abel,
the sacrifice of Abraham, our father in
   faith,
and the bread and wine offered by your
   priest Melchisedech.**

Almighty God,
we pray that your angel may take this
**   sacrifice**
to your altar in heaven.
Then, as we receive from this altar
the sacred body and blood of your Son,
let us be filled with every grace and
**   blessing.**

(Through Christ our Lord. Amen.)

Commemoration of the Dead

**Remember, Lord, those who have died
and have gone before us marked with
   the sign of faith,
especially those for whom we now pray,
   N. and N.
May these, and all who sleep in Christ,
find in your presence
light, happiness, and peace.**

(Through Christ our Lord, Amen.)

For ourselves, too, we ask
some share in the fellowship of your
    apostles and martyrs,
with John the Baptist, Stephen,
    Matthias, Barnabas,
(Ignatius, Alexander, Marcellinus,
    Peter,
Felicity, Perpetua, Agatha, Lucy,
Agnes, Cecilia, Anastasia,)
and all the saints.

Though we are sinners,
we trust in your mercy and love.
Do not consider what we truly deserve,
but grant us your forgiveness.
Through Christ our Lord
you give us all these gifts.
You fill them with life and goodness,
you bless them and make them holy.

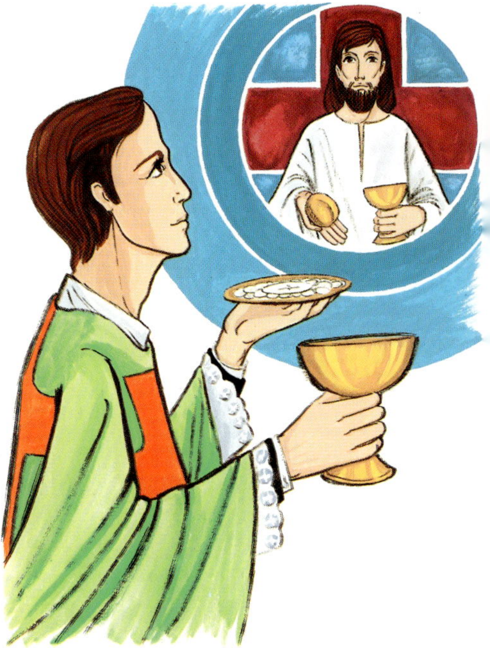

Concluding Doxology

**Through him,
with him,
in him,
in the unity of the Holy Spirit,
all glory and honor is yours,
almighty Father,
for ever and ever**

All reply: **Amen.**

COMMUNION RITE

Lord's Prayer _____

Priest: **Let us pray with confidence to the Father in the words our Savior gave us:**

Priest and people: **Our Father, who art in heaven,
hallowed be thy name;
thy kingdom come;
thy will be done on earth as it is in heaven.
Give us this day our daily bread;
and forgive us our trespasses
as we forgive those who trespass against us;
and lead us not into temptation,
but deliver us from evil.**

Priest: **Deliver us, Lord, from every evil,
and grant us peace in our day.
In your mercy keep us free from sin
and protect us from all anxiety
as we wait in joyful hope
for the coming of our Savior, Jesus Christ.**

People: **For the kingdom, the power, and the glory are yours, now and for ever.**

Sign of Peace

(The priest says the prayer for peace and concludes: **for ever and ever.***)*

People: **Amen.**

Priest: **The peace of the Lord be with you always.**

People: **And also with you.**

Deacon (or Priest):

    Let us offer each other the sign of peace.

(The people exchange a sign of peace and love, according to local custom.)

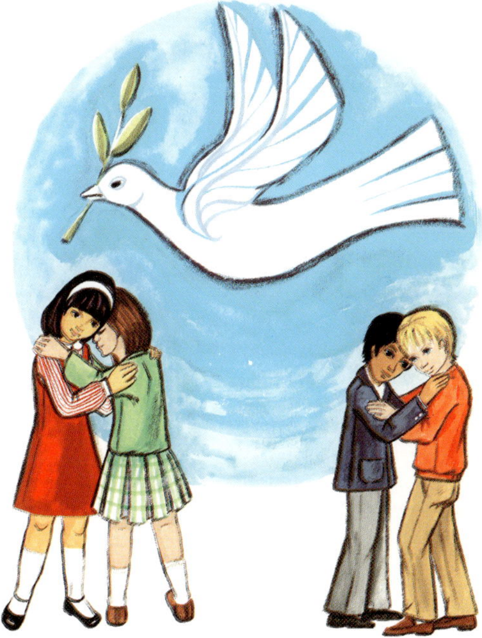

Breaking of the Bread

(The people sing or say:)

Lamb of God, you take away the sins of the world:
> **have mercy on us.**

Lamb of God, you take away the sins of the world:
> **have mercy on us.**

Lamb of God, you take away the sins of the world:
> **grant us peace.**

(Then the priest joins his hands and says quietly:)

**Lord Jesus Christ, Son of the Living God,
by the will of the Father and the work of
   the Holy Spirit
your death brought life to the world.
By your holy body and blood
free me from all my sins and from every
   evil.
Keep me faithful to your teaching,
and never let me be parted from you.**

(or)

**Lord Jesus Christ,
with faith in your love and mercy
I eat your body and drink your blood.
Let it not bring me condemnation,
but health in mind and body.**

Communion _____

Priest: **This is the Lamb of God
who takes away the sins of the world.
Happy are those who are called to his supper.**

Priest and people: **Lord, I am not worthy to receive you,
but only say the word and I shall be healed.**

The priest says quietly:

May the body of Christ bring me to everlasting life.

He reverently consumes the body of Christ. The priest then takes the chalice and says in a low voice:

May the blood of Christ bring me to everlasting life.

He reverently drinks the blood of Christ.

Communion of the Faithful _____

Priest: **The Body of Christ.**

Communicant: **Amen.**

Prayer after Communion _____

Priest: **Let us pray.**
(Everyone prays silently for a while.)

Priest: **…forever and ever.**

People: **Amen.**

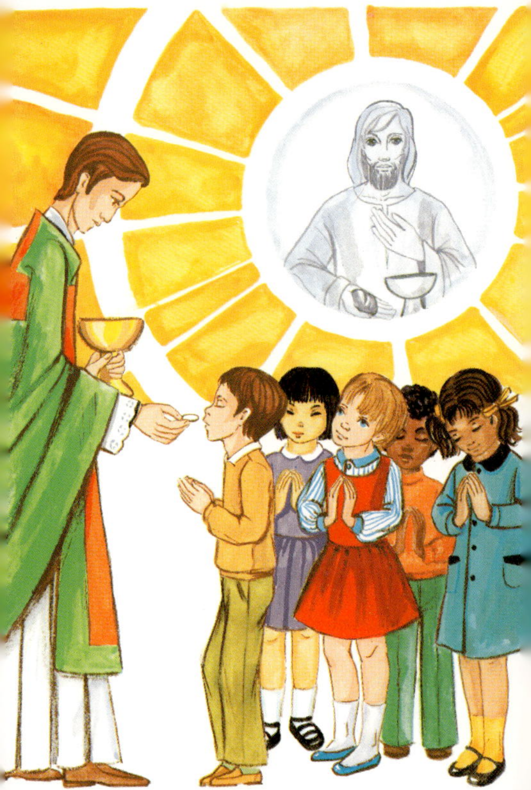

CONCLUDING RITE

Blessing

Priest: **The Lord be with you.**

People: **And also with you.**

Priest: **May almighty God bless you, the Father, and the Son, and the Holy Spirit.**

People: **Amen.**

Or a more solemn blessing or prayer over the people may be chosen by the priest. The deacon (or priest) first invites the people to bow their heads and pray for God's blessing.

The priest holds his hands outstretched toward the people to invoke God's

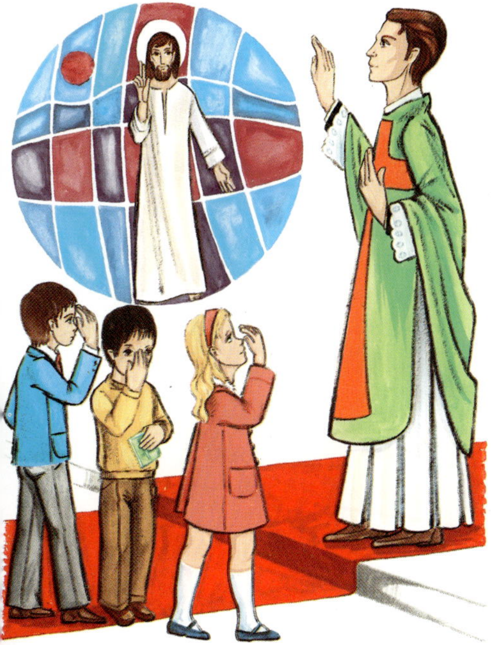

blessing upon them. The people respond Amen to each of the invocations of the solemn blessing or at the end of the prayer over the people. Then the priest concludes:

Priest: **And may the blessing of almighty God, the Father, and the Son, † and the Holy Spirit, come upon you and remain with you for ever.**

People: **Amen.**

Dismissal _____

Deacon (or priest): **Go in the peace of Christ:**

(or)
The Mass is ended, go in peace.

(or)
Go in peace to love and serve the Lord.

People: **Thanks be to God.**

Reconciliation

At one time, this sacrament was called "Penance" or "Confession". In this sacrament, the priest takes the place of Jesus. In the same way that you would tell Jesus, tell the priest you are sorry for the wrong things you have done. Before you leave, the priest will bless you and give absolution.

Examination of Conscience

Before meeting the priest, it is good to examine your life. Did you do things that were wrong? Did you omit good things that you should have done? Here are some questions you may ask yourself:

Do I think about God? Do I say thanks to Him every day for his many gifts?

Do I share with others the good things I have? My talents?

Do I ever help people who are poor, hungry or handicapped?

Do I treat fairly the boys and girls in my neighborhood and at school?

Do I speak about God with respect?

Do I respect my body and take good care of it?

Do I respect what belongs to other people?

Do I tell the truth always?

Am I willing to make up after a quarrel?

Am I willing to ask forgiveness when I hurt someone by my selfishness?

Do I really try to pray when I come to church, or do I spend time disturbing others?

Do I show my love to people who are sick or lonely?

Meeting With the Priest

When you enter the Reconciliation Room or Confessional, say "Hello Father," or greet him in some way.

First, make the Sign of the Cross. While you are doing this, the priest will be blessing you. Second, tell the priest what you have done wrong and, if necessary, why you did it. Third, listen carefully to what the priest says to you. He will usually ask you to say a prayer or to do something to show that you are sorry for your sins. He may ask you to say an Act of Contrition. Fourth, listen as the priest says the words of absolution and reconciliation.

When you are leaving, remember to say "Thank you, Father," and to either sit or kneel in the pews for a few minutes. Say your penance and be grateful, as God has forgiven you.

STORIES ABOUT JESUS

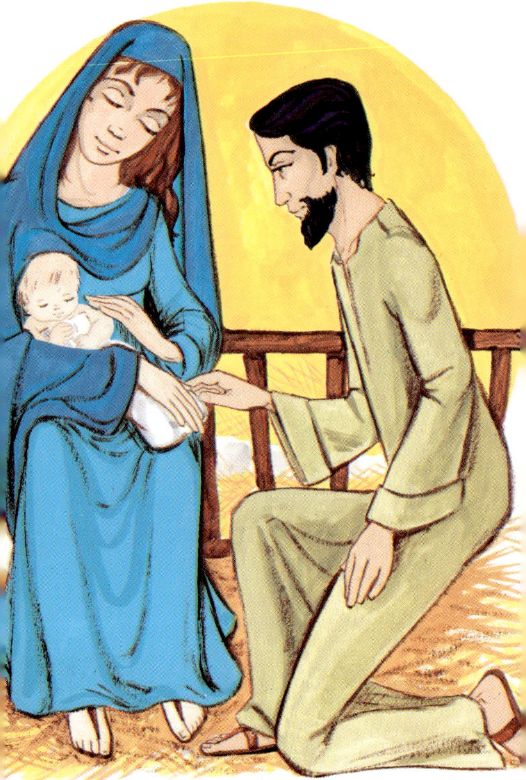

Mary's Baby

Many years ago a man named Joseph set out for Bethlehem. He took with him Mary, his wife. For three days they traveled before they reached the town. But at the inn, there was no room for Joseph and his wife. They had to sleep in a cave where farm animals were kept.

That night Mary's baby was born. She put warm things on her son. Then she laid him in a manger filled with soft straw.

Joseph loved the new baby with all his heart. He took good care of the child and of Mary, its mother.

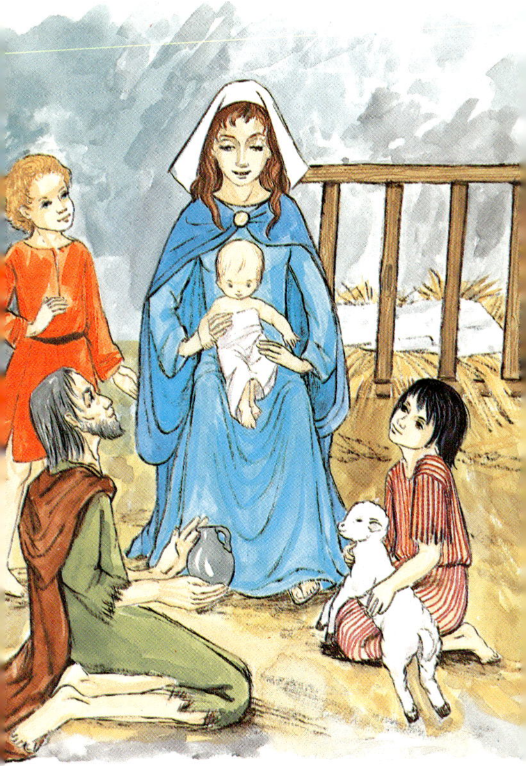

Shepherds Come at Night

That night shepherds watched in a nearby field. And an angel came and said to them, "I bring you news of great joy. In Bethlehem, a Savior has been born. You will find him sleeping in a manger."

Then many angels came. They praised God and sang, "Glory to God in the highest."

One of the shepherds cried, "Let us go to Bethlehem. Let us find this child."

The shepherds did find the baby. And they praised God for what they had seen and heard.

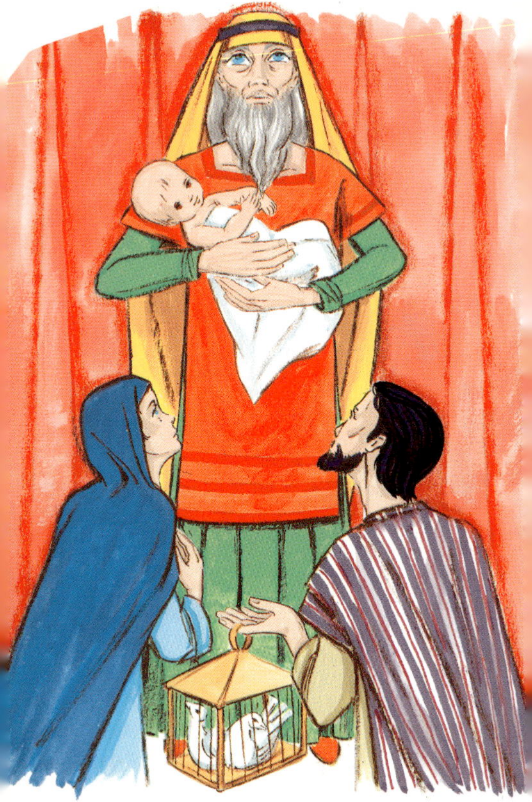

The Child Is Called Jesus

After eight days Mary and Joseph named the baby "Jesus." And they took him to the temple to offer him to God.

That day, an old man named Simeon was in the temple. He knew that God had promised to send a Savior to earth — a Savior to save the people from their sins. Each day Simeon prayed, "Let me see the Savior before I die."

Now in the temple, Simeon took Mary's baby in his arms. He thanked God, saying, "This child is the Savior. God has let me see him. Now I can die in peace."

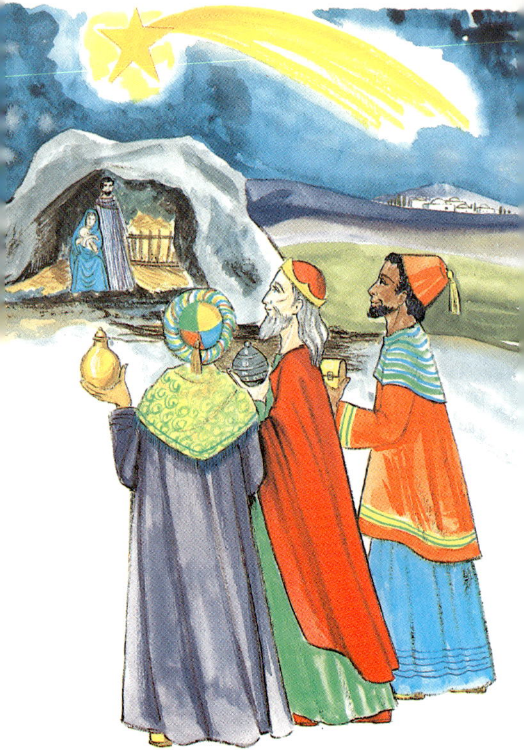

The Wise Men

In the East, three wise men saw a star crossing the sky. It was a sign that a great king had been born. The wise men followed the star till they reached Jerusalem. There they asked King Herod, "Where is the child who is born King of the Jews?"

"I do not know," said Herod. But he added, "Come back and tell me if you find him."

Again they followed the star till it stopped over the cave in Bethlehem. There the wise men adored Mary's baby and gave him gifts.

But an angel told them not to go back to King Herod. So they went home another way.

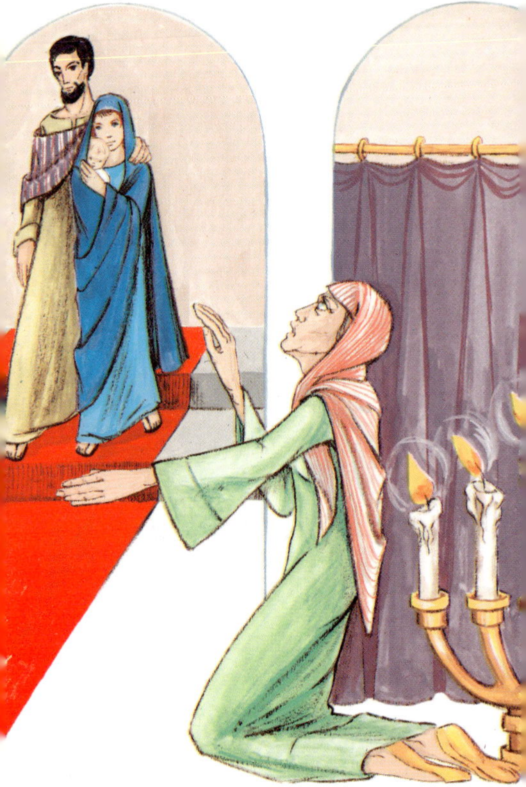

The Woman in the Temple

An old woman named Anna was in the temple that day too. She prayed God day and night to send the Savior soon.

Now she looked with wonder at the child in Mary's arms. She looked at Joseph. How poor they seemed! But Anna knew that their baby was a king. He was both king and Savior. "God has heard our prayers," said Anna. "He has sent the Savior to us."

From that day, she went about telling people the good news. "Be happy!" she would say. "Our Savior has come."

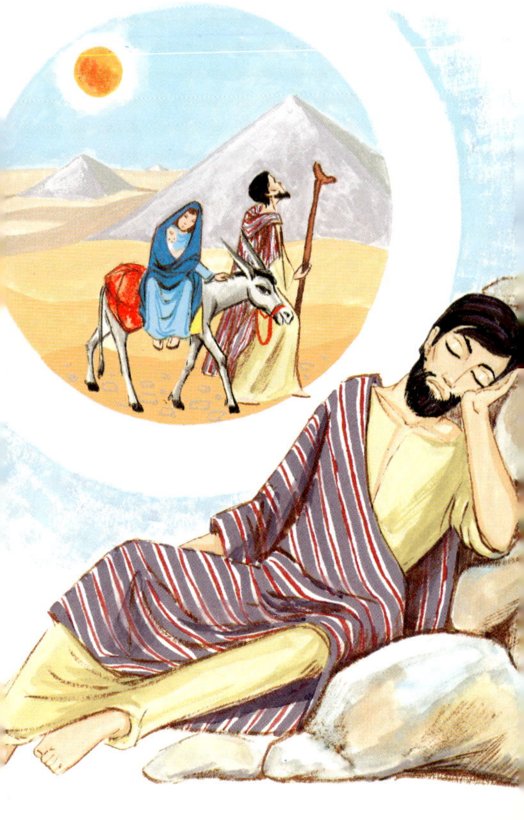

Joseph's Dream

King Herod was very angry with the wise men. How could they call a tiny baby the King of the Jews? Herod shouted to his soldiers, "I, Herod, am the only King of the Jews! Go and look for this child. If you find him, kill him."

But an angel came to Joseph in a dream. The angel said, "Take the baby and Mary, and go to Egypt. Herod wants to kill the child Jesus."

At once Joseph woke Mary. They took the baby and set out for Egypt. There they were safe.

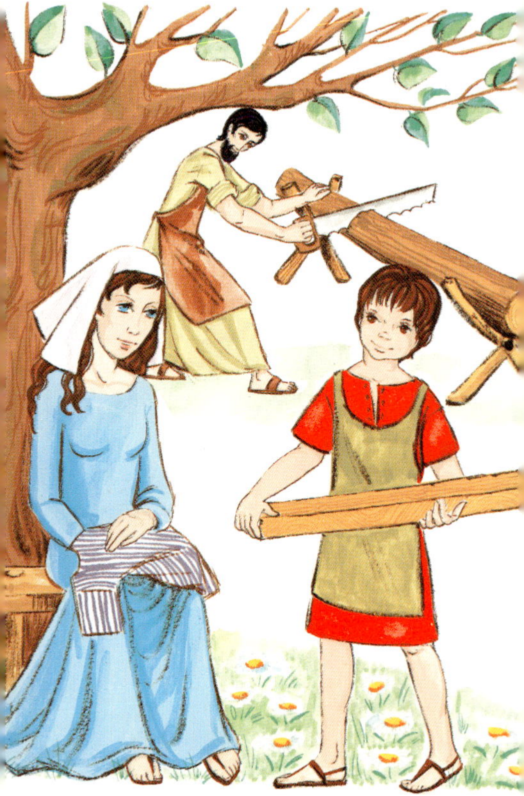

A Home for Jesus

Joseph and Mary stayed in Egypt till King Herod died. Then they started out for their own land. In the town of Nazareth, Mary and Joseph made their home. There Joseph became a carpenter, working with wood. He built houses and made tools for farmers and other workmen. He showed Jesus how to make things of wood, too.

Jesus learned to read and write, like other Jewish boys. Mary and Joseph told him about God's love for the Jews. They told him about the holy city of Jerusalem.

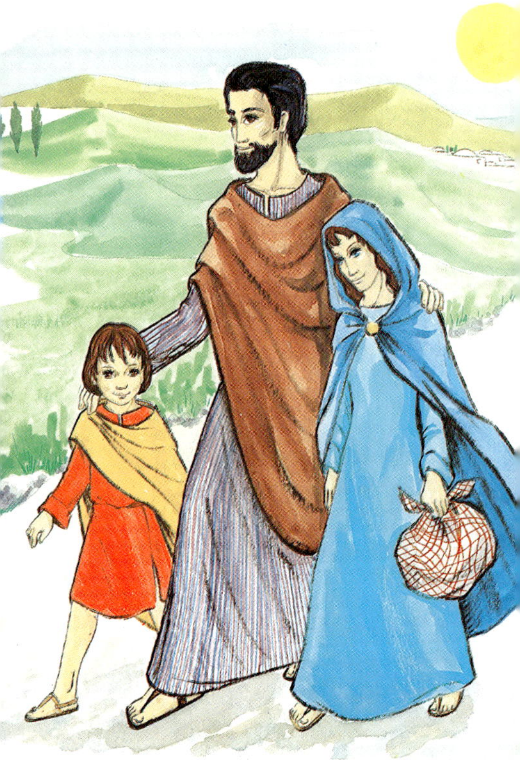

To the Holy City

Every year Joseph and Mary celebrated the Passover feast in Jerusalem. When Jesus was twelve years old, he went along with them. Sometimes he walked with Mary and the other women. Sometimes he walked with Joseph and the men.

On they went till Jesus saw, far off, the towers of Jerusalem. It was a holy city he had read about in the Bible.

But the best sight of all was Jerusalem's great temple. It was the house of God, and Jesus longed to go there.

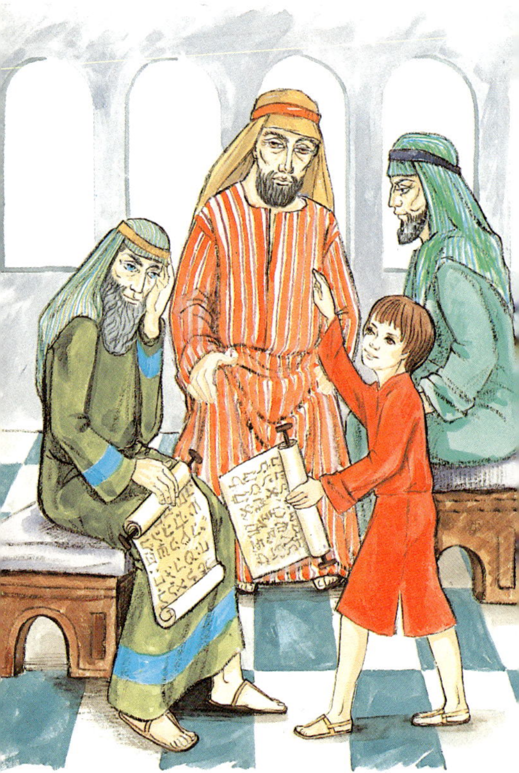

Jesus Is Lost

When the Passover was ended, Joseph and Mary started home. Mary thought Jesus was with Joseph. Joseph thought the boy was with Mary. But he was not with either one. Somehow he had been lost. Mary and Joseph looked all over. But they could not find him.

After three days they went to the temple to pray. There they found Jesus, talking about the Bible. Wise teachers listened to him.

Mary saw that her son was happy in that holy place. But he went back to Nazareth. And there he was a good son.

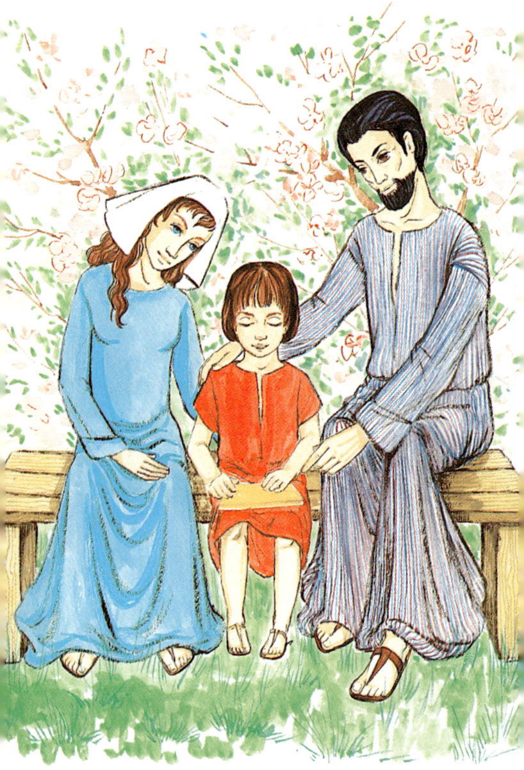

Learning the Bible

In Nazareth Jesus worked with Joseph. All day he helped in the carpenter's shop. But at night Mary and Joseph told him Bible stories.

When Jesus grew older, he went to the synagogue each day. There he learned even more about the Bible.

On Saturdays he praised God in the synagogue. There he and other people talked to God in prayer. Best of all, the teachers spoke to them about God.

Jesus loved the Bible. He loved to talk to God in prayer.

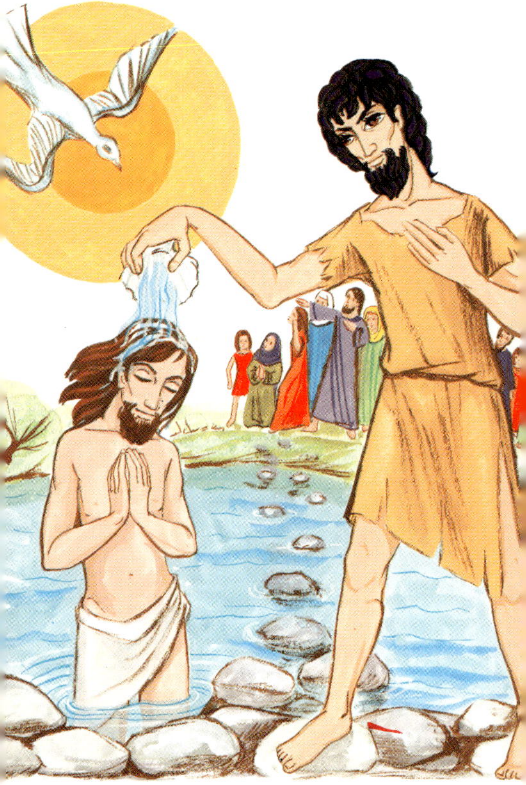

Jesus and His Cousin John

When Jesus was a man of thirty, he had news of his cousin John. John, it was said, was baptizing people in the River Jordan.

At once Jesus set out to look into this story. He walked till he came upon John standing in the river. Crowds of people were there, waiting to be baptized.

"John," said Jesus. "Baptize me."

As John the Baptist obeyed, a dove rested on Jesus' head. People heard God's voice say, "This is my son. I love him very much."

John knew then that Jesus was the Savior God had promised.

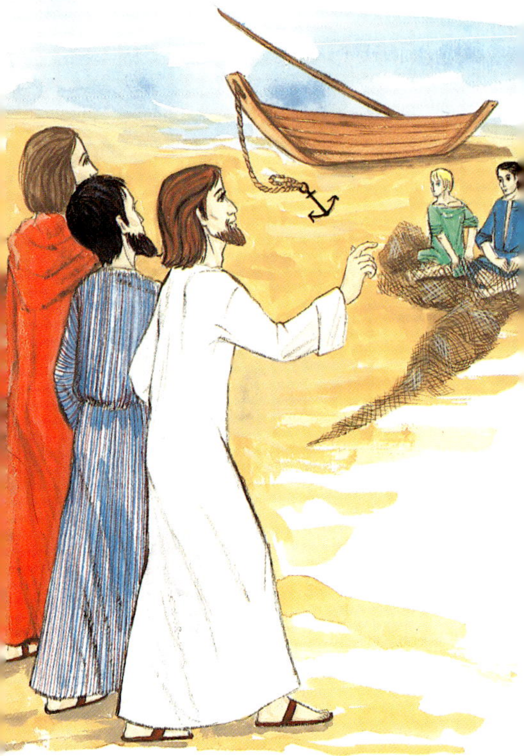

The First Apostles

One day Jesus was walking by a lake in Galilee. Out in the water, two men were fishing with nets. Jesus called, "Follow me." The two men put down their nets. They left those they loved, and they went with Jesus.

Jesus saw two more brothers, James and John. They too were casting nets, but from their father's boat. Jesus called to them over the water. They rowed the boat to shore, and they followed Jesus.

Peter and Andrew, James and John! They were the first apostles.

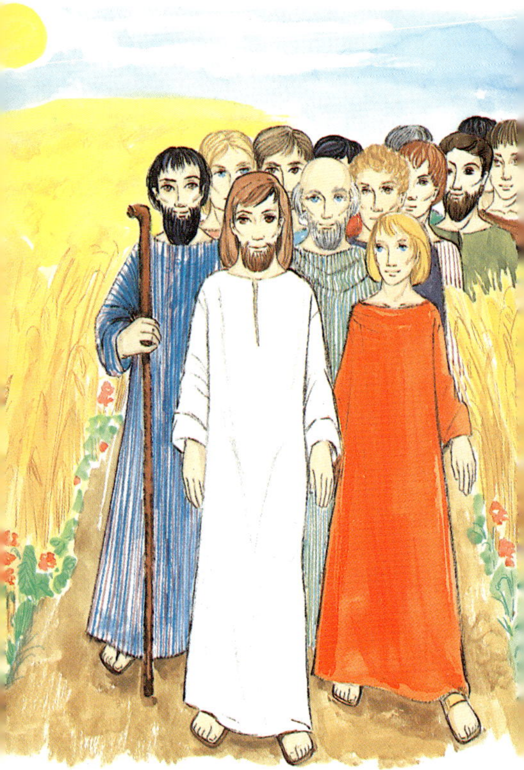

More Apostles

Later, Jesus called a man named Philip to be an apostle. He came from the same town as Peter and Andrew. In turn, Philip told one of his friends about Jesus. The two men followed the Lord.

One day Jesus saw a man taking taxes from the people. Jesus said to him, "Follow me." At once the man got up and walked with the Lord. This man was Matthew.

More men followed Jesus until there were twelve of them. They were the apostles. They were the friends of Jesus who helped him in many ways.

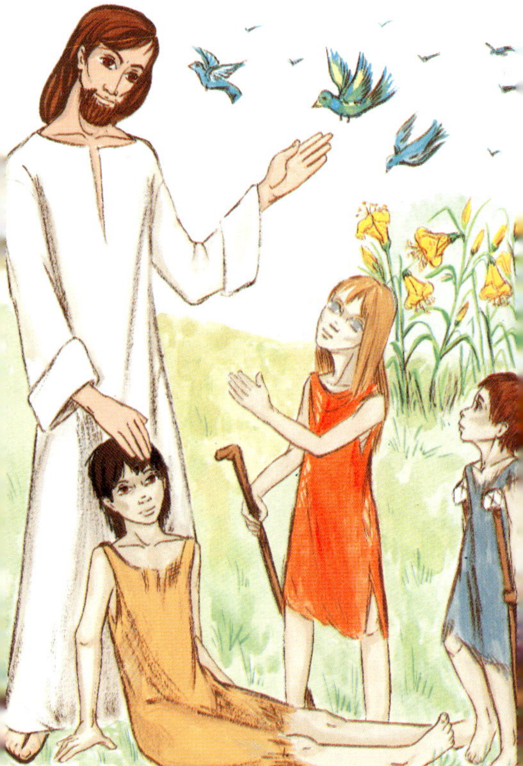

From Town to Town

The apostles walked with Jesus from town to town. In each place he stopped and talked to the people. He told them about God's love. "Look at the birds," he said. "They do no work as you do. But God takes care of them. He will take care of you, too. For you are dearer to him than all the birds."

In each town Jesus said, "Bring your sick people to me." When he touched the lame and the blind, they were cured.

Everyone wanted to see Jesus. Crowds ran into the streets to touch him and hear him. They looked at him with love.

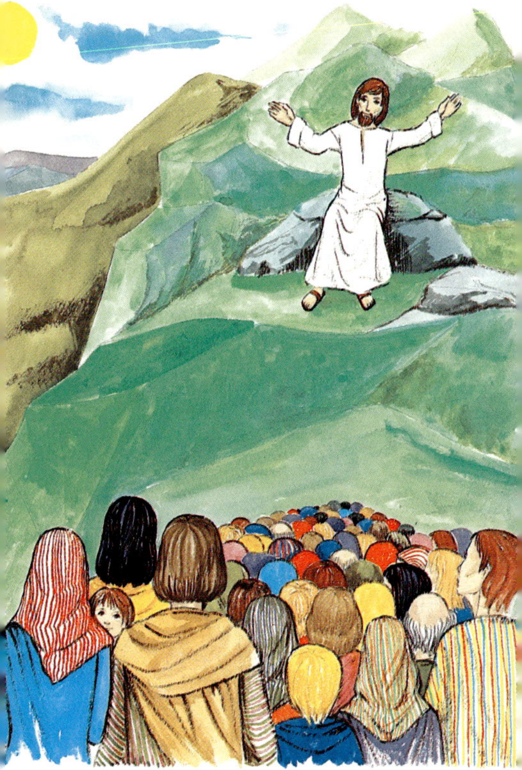

A Talk from a Mountain

A crowd followed Jesus to a country place. There he climbed up on the side of a mountain. He looked at the crowds below, and he talked to them.

He said, "Be kind to people who are not kind to you. See how kind God is. He lets the sun shine on good people and bad. You, too, must help both the good and the bad. Forgive others, and God will forgive you."

Jesus told the crowds many more things. He said, above all, they must love God and love other people.

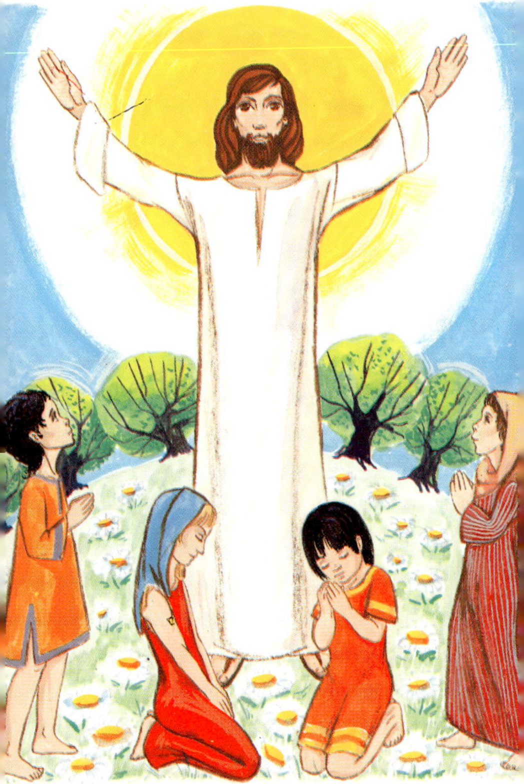

The Lord's Prayer

Jesus told the people that God is their Father. This good Father wants us to talk to him in prayer. Jesus said, "Here is how you must pray":

"Our Father, who art in heaven. Hallowed be thy name. Thy kingdom come. Thy will be done, on earth as it is in heaven. Give us this day our daily bread. And forgive us our trespasses as we forgive those who trespass against us. And lead us not into temptation, but deliver us from evil."

We call this The Lord's Prayer.

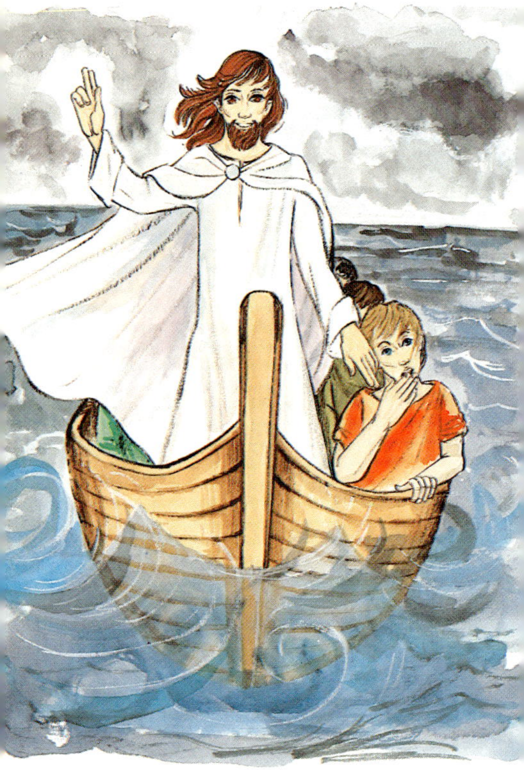

Jesus Stills the Sea

One evening Jesus was tired. And he stepped into a boat that was about to cross the lake. Lying down, he fell fast asleep. At once the wind began to blow. Big waves hit the boat. Water washed over its sides.

An apostle grew afraid. And he cried out to Jesus, who was still asleep, "Wake up Lord! The boat is about to sink!"

Jesus got up. He said to the wind and water, "Be still." At once the wind died down. The lake became still. And the apostles said, "Even the storm obeys Jesus."

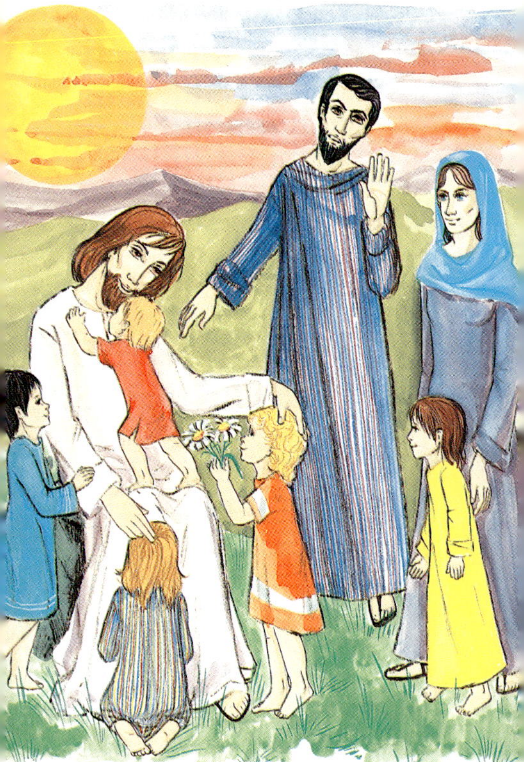

Jesus and the Children

One day some women came to Jesus. They had with them their small children. The women said to Jesus, "Please bless our little ones."

But the friends of Jesus said to the women, "Don't you see that Jesus is tired? Go away, and take your children with you."

But Jesus said to his friends, "Let the little ones come to me. Do not send them away." He laid his hands on the children to bless them.

Many times Jesus showed his great love for children.

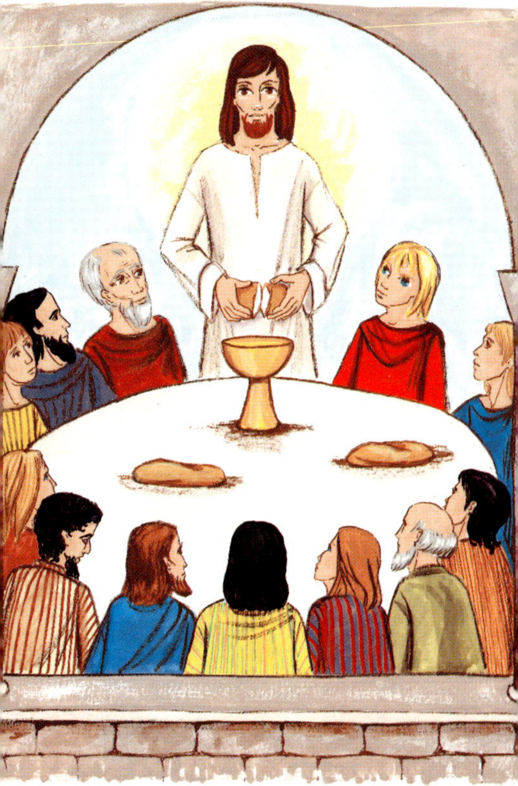

The First Mass

One Passover, Jesus sat down to supper with his apostles. During the meal he took a small, round loaf of bread. He blessed it and broke it. He gave a piece to each apostle. "Eat this," he said. "It is my body. Do this to remember me."

Then he took a cup of wine and asked for God's blessing. As he gave the cup to the apostles, he said, "Drink from the cup. It holds my blood. I shall shed my blood so that sins may be forgiven."

This supper was the first Mass. It was the first Eucharist.

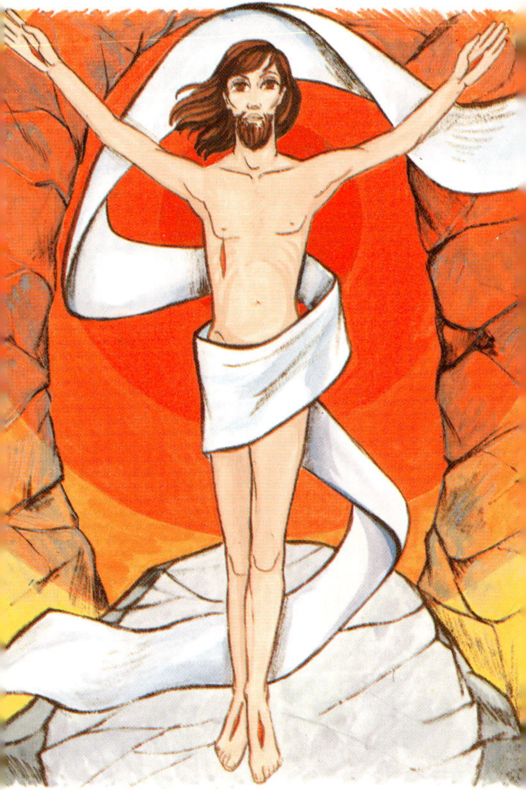

The Promises of Jesus

Most people loved Jesus. But a few did not like him. This was because the crowds followed him instead of them. And so these few had Jesus put to death. His dead body was laid in a cave called a tomb.

But Jesus came back from the dead. On Easter morning he walked out of the tomb, alive again. He stayed with his friends for about a month. Then he rose into heaven.

Jesus said that we shall see him again some day. We shall be happy with him and his Father forever.

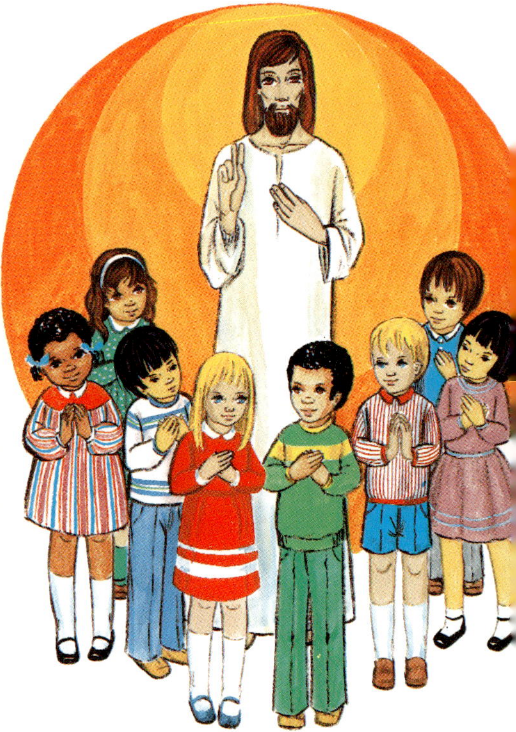

PRAYERS AND DEVOTIONS

The Sign of the Cross

"In the name of the Father
and of the Son
and of the Holy Spirit. Amen."

The Lord's Prayer

"Our Father, who art in heaven,
hallowed be thy name;
thy kingdom come;
thy will be done on earth
as it is in heaven.
Give us this day
our daily bread;
and forgive us our trespasses
as we forgive those
who trespass against us
and lead us not into temptation,
but deliver us from evil. Amen."

The Hail Mary

"Hail Mary, full of grace.
The Lord is with thee.
Blessed art thou amongst women,
and blessed is the fruit
of thy womb, Jesus.
Holy Mary, Mother of God,
pray for us sinners,
now and at the hour
of our death. Amen."

Glory Be

"Glory be to the Father,
and to the Son,
and to the Holy Spirit,
as it was in the beginning,
is now, and ever shall be,
world without end. Amen."

The Apostles' Creed

"I believe in God the Father Almighty, Creator of heaven and earth; and in Jesus Christ, His only Son, our Lord; who was conceived by the Holy Spirit, born of the Virgin Mary, suffered under Pontius Pilate, was crucified, died, and was buried; He descended into hell; the third day He arose again from the dead; He ascended into heaven, and is seated at the right hand of God the Father almighty; from thence He shall come to judge the living and the dead. I believe in the Holy Spirit; the holy Catholic Church; the Communion of Saints; the forgiveness of sins; the resurrection of the body; and life everlasting. Amen."

Here is a prayer to Mary, the Mother of Jesus. In it, we beg her to pray for us.

Memorare

"**Remember, O most loving Virgin Mary,
That never was it known that anyone who asked for your protection, or looked for your aid, or begged for your prayers, was left without help. As I think of this, I fly to you, O Virgin of Virgins, my Mother. To you I go, before you I kneel, filled with sorrow for my sins. Do not turn away from me, O Mother of Jesus, but hear me and pray for me to your son. Amen.**"

Morning Prayer

In the morning we thank God for keeping us safe all night. We thank him for the new day. We offer him everything we shall do and say and think.

A Morning Offering

"O Jesus, I offer you everything
I shall do and say and think today.
I offer you my happy times
and my sad times.
I offer them so that all you want
may come to pass.
I join my prayers to those of Mary,
your Mother, who is my mother, too."

At Playtime

God wants us to be happy. When playtime comes, he wants us to enjoy it. Playtime should be a happy time for us and our friends. And so we ask God to help us to be fair during our games. We offer him the fun we shall have while we play.

Before Meals

"Bless us, O Lord,
and these your gifts,
which we are about to receive
from your goodness,
through Christ, our Lord.
May the Lord relieve the wants
of others. Amen."

Night Prayers

Before we go to bed, we thank God for the day that is past. We ask him to bless all the people we love. We tell God we are sorry for any wrong we have done. We may say the Act of Contrition. We also may ask God to give us a good night's sleep and say the following prayer:

A Prayer at Bedtime

"Be a light to us, O Lord God. Drive away all harm this night, and keep us safe in your love. Through our Lord Jesus Christ. Amen."

Act of Contrition

"O my God,
I am heartily sorry
for having offended You,
and I detest all my sins,
because of Your just punishments,
but most of all
because they offend You, my God,
who are all good
and deserving of all love.
I firmly resolve,
with the help of Your grace,
to sin no more
and to avoid the near occasions
of sin. Amen."

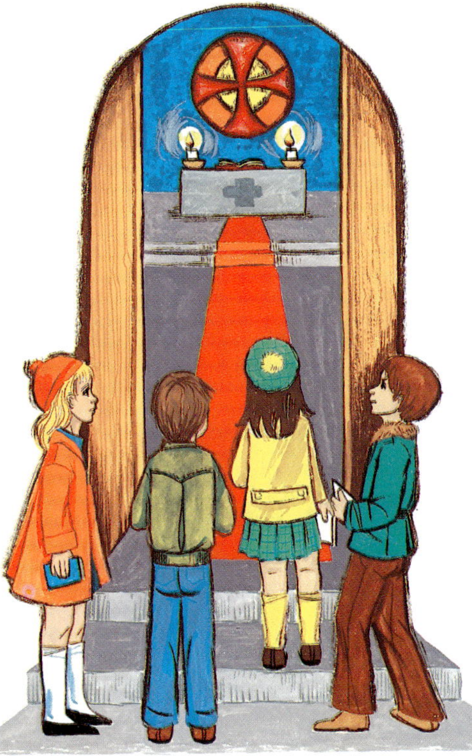

Talking to God

God is everywhere, and we can always talk to him. Talking to God is praying. Thinking about God is praying.

God gave us all we have, and so we say or think,
"Thank you, God."

We praise him,
"I love you God. I adore you."

We tell him we are sorry for not being kind, and we say,
"I will try to be more loving."

We ask God to help us.
"Teach me to tell the truth. Help me to do well in school." We talk to God, and then we are quiet. He may answer us by sending ideas and thoughts to help us.

Our friends don't always want the things we want. But sometimes they go along with us. Sometimes we go along with them. That is how everyone gets a chance. But being fair is not always easy, and so we ask God to help us.

When I Don't Get My Own Way

"Dear Lord, my friends
 were against me today.
I wanted to play one game.
They wanted to play another.
I didn't like that.
I went away and sat alone.
But that wasn't much fun, either.
Lord, help me to love my friends.
Help me to see things their way
 once in a while.
Don't let me always think about myself.
Help me to be a true friend."

Sometimes we spoil things that belong to others. We write on their walls and fences. We pull up their plants and flowers. We even break other children's toys and tear their books.

When I Spoil What Belongs to Others

"O Lord, I just painted words
 on a fence across the street.
I thought it was a funny thing to do.
But now I'm sorry.
I spoiled what isn't mine,
 and that's a kind of stealing.
Lord, help me to be careful
 of what belongs to others.
Help me to think before
 I do mean and silly things.
Help me to keep the world
 a clean, good place to live."

Our parents tell us to do things that will help us. They want us to learn all we can. They want us to be healthy. They want us to grow up to be good and happy people. But sometimes what our parents want isn't what we want.

When It's Hard to Obey

"Lord, now and then it's hard
   to do what my parents ask of me.
I don't always want to turn off
   the TV when I'm told.
I don't always feel like doing
   my homework.
I don't always want to eat
   what Mother says is good for me.
Lord, help me to remember
   that my parents only want to help me.
You put them over me, Lord.
Help me to obey."

God gave everyone some gift. One of us is good at games. Another is good at school work. Still another makes people smile and feel happy.

When Other People Are Praised

"Dear Lord, I felt cross today
   when my friend was praised.
He painted a picture in school,
   and everyone said it was good.
I didn't like that.
Help me to be happy when I hear
   good things about a friend.
Remind me that he is being praised
   for using your gift.
Let me make good use of your gift
   to me.
It may be small, but it came from you.
Thank you, Lord."

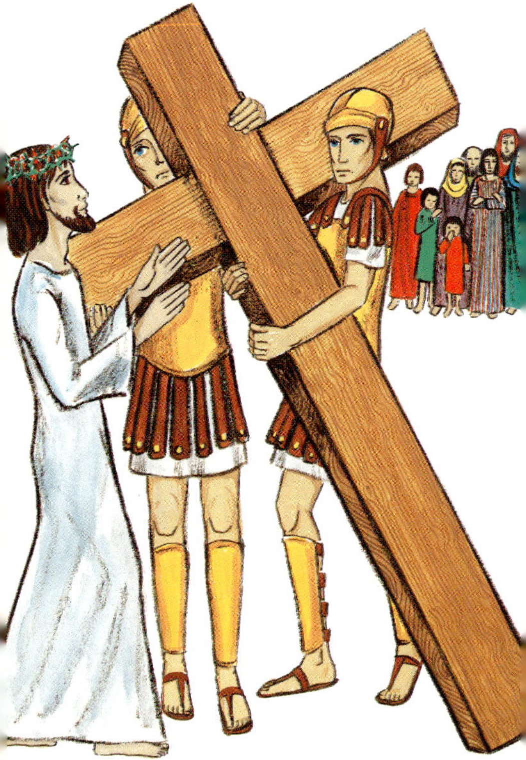

The Stations of the Cross

The story is told that after Jesus ascended to heaven, his mother Mary retraced the steps of her son's passion. From time to time she would walk from the governor's house to Calvary along the same path taken by Jesus.

It is a good way to show Jesus how thankful we are for all he has done for us.

In your church you will see fourteen pictures around the walls. On each picture there is a cross and a number. The pictures, or stations, show Jesus on his way to Calvary. They show his death and burial. We walk from one station to another. We stop at each one. We think of what is happening in the picture. We do not have to say any prayers.

1st Station

Jesus Is Condemned to Death.

Jesus is brought before Pilate to be judged. He is innocent but he is condemned and taken away to be put to death.

2nd Station

Jesus Takes Up His Cross.

The cross is very heavy. Jesus knows it will be painful but he accepts it willingly to save us from our sins.

3rd Station

Jesus Falls for the First Time.

The heavy cross drives the thorns still deeper into his brow and Jesus is weak from loss of blood. He falls and the soldiers roughly drag him up again.

4th Station

Jesus Meets His Mother.

When Mary sees Jesus, her heart is broken. He is covered with dirt and blood. Mary weeps because he is suffering terribly and there is no way she can help him.

5th Station

Simon of Cyrene Helps Jesus.

Jesus is so weak he can no longer carry the cross. The soldiers fear that he will faint or die on the way. So they ask a man named Simon to help him.

6th Station

Veronica Wipes the Face of Jesus.

A good lady runs to Jesus and wipes his face with her veil. How she pitied him and how anxious she was to do something for him!

7th Station
Jesus Falls the Second Time.

Again Jesus staggers under the weight of the cross and falls heavily to the ground. The cruel soldiers, with kicks and blows, force him to his feet again.

8th Station
Jesus Meets the Women of Jerusalem.

Jesus meets some women who are grieving and crying loudly. He tells them not to weep for him but for all the sinners who will not repent and be saved.

9th Station
Jesus Falls the Third Time.

Jesus is now near the place where he will be fastened to the cross. He thinks of all the pain he must still suffer. All his strength leaves him and he falls to the earth.

10th Station
Jesus is Stripped of His Clothes.

The long journey to Calvary is now finished. The soldiers roughly tear off his clothes. Jesus is humiliated and treated like a common criminal.

11th Station
Jesus is Nailed to the Cross.

At last, Jesus is placed upon the cross. The soldiers then drive nails through his hands and feet. The cross is then raised and placed into the earth.

12th Station
Jesus Dies on the Cross.

How patiently Jesus suffers. For three long hours his body hangs on the cross. He speaks kindly to the good thief. He lovingly talks to Mary. At last he bows his head and dies.

13th Station

The Body of Jesus Is Taken Down from the Cross.

After his death, friends take Jesus down from the cross. Gently they lower his body into the arms of his mother, Mary. With great love she again holds her beloved son.

14th Station

The Body of Jesus Is Laid in the Tomb.

The body of Jesus is placed in a tomb. Soldiers seal the tomb and block the entrance with a great stone. The followers of Jesus return to their homes to wait for Jesus to rise from the dead on the third day, as he promised.

The Rosary

The Rosary is made up of sets, or groups, of beads on a chain. In each set there are one big bead and ten small beads. Each set is called a dècade.

On the big beads, we say the Our Father. On the small beads, we say the Hail Mary. After the last Hail Mary in a decade, we say a Glory Be. Before each decade, we think of something that happened to Jesus and Mary.

The Joyful Mysteries

1. The Annunciation
2. The Visitation
3. The Birth of Jesus
4. The Presentation of Jesus in the Temple.

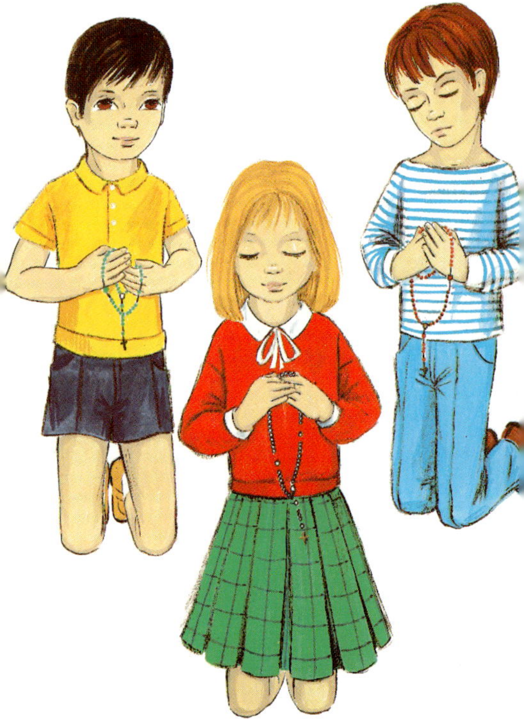

5. The Finding of Jesus in the Temple.

The Sorrowful Mysteries

1. The Agony in the Garden
2. The Scourging of Jesus
3. The Crowning of Jesus with Thorns
4. The Carrying of the Cross
5. The Death of Jesus on the Cross

The Glorious Mysteries

1. The Resurrection
2. The Ascension
3. The Coming of the Holy Spirit
4. The Assumption of Mary
5. The Coronation of Mary in Heaven

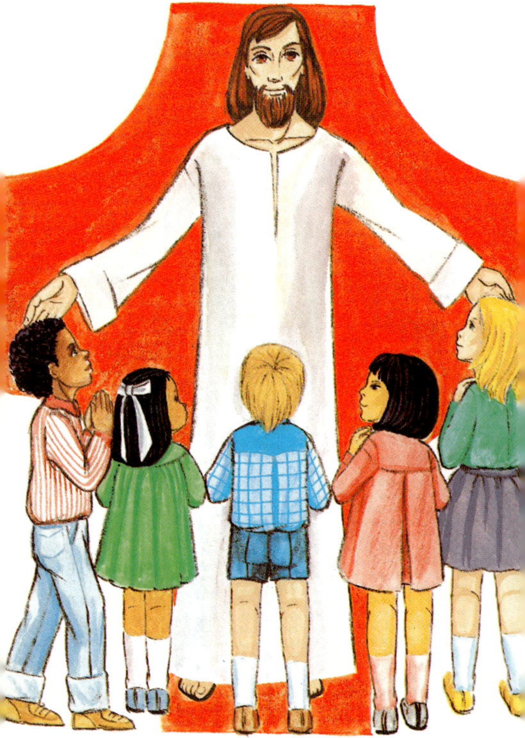

FOLLOWING JESUS IN OUR LIVES

The Ten Commandments

1. I, the Lord, am your God. You shall not have other gods besides me.
2. You shall not take the name of the Lord, your God, in vain.
3. Remember to keep holy the sabbath day.
4. Honor your father and your mother.
5. You shall not kill.
6. You shall not commit adultery.
7. You shall not steal.
8. You shall not bear false witness against your neighbor.
9. You shall not covet your neighbor's wife.
10. You shall not covet anything that belongs to your neighbor.

The Beatitudes

1. Blessed are the poor in spirit, for the kingdom of heaven is theirs.
2. Blessed are those who are sad, for they shall be comforted.
3. Blessed are the mild and gentle, for they shall inherit the land.
4. Blessed are those who hunger and thirst for justice, for they shall be filled.
5. Blessed are the merciful, for they shall receive mercy.
6. Blessed are the pure in heart, for they shall see God.
7. Blessed are those who make peace, for they shall be called the children of God.
8. Blessed are those who suffer for my sake, for heaven will be theirs.

What the Church Asks of Us

1. That we go to Mass on Sundays and holy days of obligation.

2. That we fast and abstain on the days appointed.

3. That we confess our sins at least once a year.

4. That we receive Holy Communion during the Easter time.

5. That we contribute to the support of the Church.

6. That we observe the laws of the Church on marriage.

The Sacraments

The seven sacraments are special ways established by Jesus to help us live God's life more fully. Each sacrament brings with it a special grace from God.

They are:
1. Baptism
2. Confirmation
3. Holy Eucharist
4. Reconciliation
5. Anointing of the Sick
6. Holy Orders
7. Matrimony

Virtues
God's Gifts to Us

Faith—we believe all that God tells us.

Hope—we trust that God will always help us.

Love—we love God and all people.

Gifts of the Holy Spirit

Wisdom	Knowledge
Understanding	Piety
Counsel	Fear of
Fortitude	the Lord

The Chief Corporal Works of Mercy

To feed the hungry.

To give drink to the thirsty.

To clothe the naked.

To visit the imprisoned.

To shelter the homeless.

To visit the sick.

To bury the dead.

Jesus said: "As long as you did it for one of these, the least of my brethren, you did it to Me."

The Chief Spiritual Works of Mercy

To admonish the sinner.

To instruct the ignorant.

To counsel the doubtful.

To comfort the sorrowful.

To bear wrongs patiently.

To forgive all injuries.

To pray for the living and the dead.

Jesus said: "Judge not, and you will not be judged; condemn not, and you will not be condemned; forgive, and you will be forgiven."

The Divine Praises

"Blessed be God.
Blessed be his Holy Name.
Blessed be Jesus Christ,
   true God and true Man.
Blessed be the name of Jesus.
Blessed be his most Sacred Heart.
Blessed be his most Precious Blood.
Blessed be Jesus in the most
   Holy Sacrament of the altar.
Blessed be the Holy Spirit,
   the Paraclete.
Blessed be the great Mother of God,
   Mary most holy.
Blessed be her holy and Immaculate
   Conception.
Blessed be her glorious Assumption.
Blessed be Joseph her most
   chaste spouse.
Blessed be God in his angels
   and in his saints."

Prayer of St. Francis of Assisi

"Lord, make me an instrument of your peace.
Where there is hatred, let me sow love;
Where there is injury, your pardon;
Where there is doubt, faith;
Where there is despair, hope;
Where there is darkness, light;
And where there is sadness, joy.
O Divine Master, grant that I may not so much seek to be consoled as to console; to be understood as to understand; to be loved as to love. For it is in giving that we receive, it is in pardoning that we are pardoned, and it is in dying that we are born to eternal life."